COASTERS in 2008
by
Bernard McCall

INTRODUCTION

Welcome to the ninth in this series of what have become known as the "coaster annuals".

This volume sees two changes. Firstly, we have added the word "in" to the title. This is to help the retail trade which seems to have difficulty in coping with the concept of a retrospective book. Secondly, we have abandoned the requirement to use two photographs from each week of the year. That was becoming an unhelpful constraint which meant that some excellent photographs were being omitted. So this time, the images take us sequentially through the year. We feel that readers will want to see a varied collection of coasters in a wide range of locations. There is no real need to limit the choice by date.

Thanks to all the photographers who have submitted images for possible inclusion in the book.

Again there is an impression that the frequency of name changes during the year is diminishing. That seemed to reach a peak in *Coasters 2006*.

Acknowledgements

I always comment that a book such as this could not be written without the help of many individuals and sources. Special thanks must go to the many photographers who have submitted material for possible inclusion in the book. There are some individuals who have always been ready to answer any question put to them. I feel that special mention must be made of Krispen Atkinson, Adrian Brown, Gert Uwe Detlefsen, Bert Kruidhof, Bent Mikkelsen, Richard Potter, Michael Pryce and Oliver Sesemann in this context. Gil Mayes has, as always, been a constant source of support and advice; he has also read the proofs and suggested many wise alterations. Any errors which remain are my own responsibility, and I do apologise for any there may be. I also want to place on record my thanks to the staff of Amadeus Press for their contribution to the finished book.

Bernard McCall

Portishead, March 2009

Copyright © 2009 by Bernard McCall. The right of Bernard McCall to be identified as author of this work has been asserted by him in accordance with the Copyright, Design and Patent Act 1998.

All rights reserved. No part of this publication may be reproduced, stored in a retrieval system or transmitted in any form or by any means (electronic, digital, mechanical, photocopying, recording or otherwise) without prior permission of the publisher.

Published by Bernard McCall, 400 Nore Road, Portishead, Bristol, BS20 8EZ, England. Website : www.coastalshipping.co.uk
Telephone/fax : 01275 846178.   E-mail : bernard@coastalshipping.co.uk
All distribution enquiries should be addressed to the publisher.

Printed by Amadeus Press, Ezra House, West 26 Business Park, Cleckheaton, West Yorkshire, BD19 4TQ
Telephone : 01274 863210; fax : 01274 863211; e-mail : info@amadeuspress.co.uk; website : www.amadeuspress.co.uk

ISBN : 978-1-902953-40-3

Above : "The Sky at Night". Sometimes a photograph provides its own caption and this is a fine example. The **Arklow Sky** (NLD, 2316gt/98) is seen at the Wash port of Boston on the evening of 27 October. Launched on 31 March 2000, she is one of seven similar vessels built between 1995 and 2000 for Arklow Shipping at the Barkmeijer Shipyard in Stroobos. None of the vessels sails under the Irish flag; five are registered in the Netherlands and the remaining two in the Bahamas. She had arrived from Lübeck and was waiting to load wheat for Drogheda. The Wash port of Boston in Lincolnshire has enjoyed increases in trade over recent years. It is ideally placed to serve the agricultural hinterland in addition to local manufacturing industries.

(David Dixon)

Front cover : Manchester Docks have changed beyond recognition in the last 20 years and those changes will continue with a new BBC centre being built in the background of this photograph. Now owned by The Big Ditch Shipping Company, the newly-refurbished **Gina D** (507gt/75), ex **Yeoman Rose**-99, **Island Swift**-90, **Seaborne Trader**-87, is moored in one of the former drydocks as she awaits discharge of a cargo of grain brought from Liverpool for the nearby Rank Hovis mill. These are the only cargoes brought regularly to this section of the Canal.

(Bernard McCall)

The **Swedica Hav** (BHS, 1616gt/86) is a typical product of the Hugo Peters shipyard in Wewelsfleth. Initially named **Jan Meeder**, she was launched on 26 March 1986 and handed over to owner Kapitän Frank Gottron on 3 May. Sold to Kapitän Bernd Wittkowski on 11 March 1997, she was renamed **Sea Weser** for the duration of a time charter to Seacon. Following sale to Norwegian owners in January 2001, she became **Ophir** and then **Swedica Hav** in early September 2006 when she became part of the steadily-growing fleet of Bergen-based Hav Ship Management. We see her in the River Mersey as she approaches Eastham locks on 12 January almost at the end of a voyage from San Ciprian to Runcorn. She sailed late the following day to Glasgow.

(Alan Faulkner)

The **Shetland Trader** (BRB, 1512gt/92) is the sixth vessel to have carried this name. She appeared in *Coasters 2006* under her previous name of **Lass Mars**. There we noted that she was the second in a series of five sisterships built at the Rosslauerwerft shipyard on the River Elbe. She was launched as **Mars** but delivered to her German owners as **Lass Mars** in May 1992. All five of these ships have now come into the ownership of Faversham Ships Ltd, the **Lass Mars** being the first to be handed over in the summer of 2007. There is no doubt that the ships look far better in the dark-blue hull colours of their British owners. With a dramatic backdrop of the barren landscape of Islay, the **Shetland Trader** approaches Port Ellen on 16 January with a full cargo of barley for the whisky distilleries on the island.

(Elliott Bowman)

The Danish tanker operator Herning Tankers has had a varied and modern fleet for many years and has always been ready to invest in new ships. Latterly, many of these have come from shipyards in Turkey. On 22 January the **Hanne Theresa** (DIS, 2682gt/02), ex **Laila Theresa**-02, was photographed as she headed down the New Waterway from Rotterdam. Built by R.M.K. Tersanesi at Tuizla, she is the first of several Turkish-built tankers to appear in this volume. She has twelve tanks with a total capacity of 4528 cubic metres and is fitted with cargo heating coils. She is powered by a 4-stroke 8-cylinder MaK engine of 3263bhp.

(Koos Goudriaan)

As we comment elsewhere, Dutch shipyards have continued to build coasters in recent years, this success being due to several factors. One important factor has been the ability to identify a niche market and build a series of standard ships to fit that niche. A good example is the **Hydra** (NLD, 2281gt/07) which is the first example of a class known as the Bijlsma Trader 3250 class which is expected to have at least 18 examples in due course. Her hull was built by Lodenice Nova, at Melnik, and she was completed at the Bijlsma shipyard in Lemmer. Handed over to her two captain/owners at Delfzijl on 7 September 2007, she is managed by Wagenborg.

(Dick Richards)

The *Vedrey Hallarna* (GIB, 1207gt/05), ex *Pulathane*-07, outward bound in the River Thames on 20 January, is another tanker to have been constructed in Turkey, her builders being Turkter Tersane ve Deniz at Tuzla near Istanbul. In February 2007, she was acquired by Svithoid Tankers, a Swedish company which grew rapidly from August 2005. By the end of 2008, however, the company had collapsed and gone into administration. This tanker illustrates perfectly some of the complexities of modern shipping with ownership being registered to Rederi AB Väderötank but the ship being bareboat chartered by Atlantic Winds Shipping Co Ltd which is wholly owned by Svithoid Tankers. She was employed under a Contract of Affreightment to Diester Industrie, one of the largest European producers of biodiesel.

(Krispen Atkinson)

The small port of St Sampsons on the island of Guernsey is one of the few around the coast of the UK where tankers discharge their cargo whilst aground. Here we see the *Alacrity* (1930gt/90) making her final visit to the port on 27 January with a cargo of motor spirit, kerosene and derv from Milford Haven. She was built at Lowestoft by Richards (Shipbuilders) Ltd and *Lloyd's Register* notes that she is strengthened for loading and discharging whilst aground, thus making her eminently suitable for ports such as St Sampsons. After leaving St Sampsons, she sailed to Falmouth in readiness for handing over to Greek owners by whom she was renamed *Aegean VIII*. Deliveries to St Sampsons were taken over by a Svithoid tanker but the collapse of this company later in the year compelled the States of Guernsey to buy two Svithoid tankers in order to safeguard deliveries to Guernsey. Had these tankers been sold for trading elsewhere, it would have been difficult to find other suitable vessels. This is the inevitable consequence of the increased size of tankers built for coastal trades.

(Peter Stewart)

The **Clipper Beaune** (MLT, 2865gt/05) was built at the Rousse shipyard in Bulgaria as **Crescent Beaune** for Crescent Marine Services Ltd. This company had been taken over by the Clipper Group in Denmark and the tanker was renamed **Clipper Beaune** at Hull in mid-December 2007. Our photograph shows her at the Bull Anchorage in the Humber estuary on 2 February. She had left Immingham late on 29 January and did not depart from the anchorage until the early hours of 6 February when she set off for Teesport. In early August, she took up bunkering duties at Falmouth.

(John B Hood)

Sometimes there are radical design innovations which are successful, but there are some that are less than successful, at least initially. At first glance, the **RMS Kiel** (ATG, 2569gt/07) would appear to come into the latter category. The innovative design is known as the "Futura Carrier" and one of many special features is that it features modular components. It is also environmentally friendly in terms of fuel consumption and exhaust emissions. The **RMS Kiel** was the prototype and of the anticipated construction cost of €6.8 million, the German Ministry for the Environment gave a grant of €2.2 million. Construction at the Con-Mar shipyard in Brake was delayed because of the yard's financial problems and her planned launch in December 2005 had to be deferred until October 2006. Her launch on 5 October was almost a disaster when she failed to move down the slipway at the former Lühring shipyard. When two tugs were attached, she listed to port and was in danger of breaking her back before a larger tug was summoned and she was eventually pulled into the Weser. She was then towed to Wilhelmshaven for completion by Navitek Schiffsreparatur. It was planned that she should serve the RMS link between Duisburg and Goole but she rarely did and we see her on 7 February during one of her infrequent calls. In mid-2008 she was sold and renamed **Futura Carrier** under the flag of Slovakia.

(Andrew Kitchen)

The Dutch shipbuilding industry continues to build coastal vessels in considerable numbers. One of the most successful yards is that of the Barkmeijer company in Stroobos. On 8 February our photographer was on hand to capture the launch of the **Saffier** (NLD, 3970gt/08) which was designed by the yard. Although only 99,99 metres long, the ship was a deadweight of 6050 tonnes. A particularly notable feature is her box hold that is 66 metres in length, unusually long for a vessel of her size. The purpose of this is to allow her to carry wind farm equipment, cranes and other project cargoes. She can, of course, carry conventional cargoes such as forest products, steel, and bulk goods such as grain for which she has been fitted with movable bulkheads. She was handed over to owners De Bock Maritiem on 11 April and her commercial managers are Wagenborg.

(Koos Goudriaan)

Although we often see coasters of the Hammann & Prahm fleet in our annuals, it is the first time that we have included the **Selene Prahm** (DEU, 1584gt/94). She is the forerunner of three similar vessels built at the Kötter Werft shipyard in Haren/Ems for her Wischhafen-based owners. She entered service in June 1994. For the first part of her career, she was managed by Leafe and Hawkes in Hull but latterly has been on time charter to RMS. This charter ends in April 2009. We see her arriving at Grovehurst Jetty in The Swale on 8 February at the end of a voyage from Hamburg. She was bringing a cargo of raw material for the nearby factory of Knauf UK Ltd which manufactures plasterboard, acoustic boards and dry mortar for internal plaster.

(Kevin Bassett)

The **Antares** (NLD, 1172gt/84) was built at the Tille shipyard in Kootstertille. She was launched on 8 August 1984 and handed over on 4 September having successfully completed trials the previous day. Initially named **Oldehove**, she was sold in mid-1994 and spent most of the summer that year undergoing repairs at Harlingen. She was renamed **Antares** in early August and retained that name when sold within the Netherlands in early January 2005. She is seen at Gunness Wharf on the River Trent on 10 February and she departed to Rotterdam on the evening tide of the next day.

(David Dixon)

It was in 1912 that Charles M Willie & Co began business in South Wales as exporters of coal and importers of timber to be used as pit props. The shipping company was established in 1938 to handle the growing quantity of exports. Timber and forest products, mainly imported from the Iberian peninsula, have continued to play an important part in the company's trade. In recent years, the company has steadily renewed its fleet often acquiring groups of sisterships. Such a policy is ideal for maintenance purposes and for standardisation of equipment and spare parts. In mid-2006, five Sietas Type 130 ships were bought from a German owner, one of these being the **Wahlstedt** (DEU, 2568gt/85), ex **Hampoel**-02, **Wahlstedt**-97, **Monika Ehler**-95. Renamed **Celtic Endeavour** after purchase by the Willie company, she was transferred to British registry with Cardiff as her port of registry. We see her leaving Glasson Dock on 10 February at the start of a voyage to Aveiro with cullet (fragmented glass).

(C J Tabarin)

The **Whitspray** (899gt/69) was photographed as she entered Portsmouth harbour on 12 February. This small tanker now operates as a bunkering vessel in the Solent. She was built to trade in the Bristol Channel distributing refined products usually from Swansea to ports such as Bridgwater and Gloucester. She was part of the Bowker & King fleet of small estuarial tankers that operated in several parts of England. Appropriately named **Bristolian**, she was built at the Erlenbach shipyard of Bayerische Schiffbauges. mbH vom Anton Schellenberger and she was lengthened in 1971. In 1993 she was sold to John H Whitaker (Tankers) Ltd and initially worked in south-east England but was subsequently transferred to the Solent.

(Colin Drayson)

As we have said in previous annuals, trade to the upper reaches of the Manchester Ship Canal is sadly neglected. Attempts to revive this trade have met only moderate success. There have been occasional shipments of compressed timber board from Rostock in recent years. Having delivered such a cargo the **Neptun** (GIB, 2039gt/88) approaches Irlam Locks on her way back down the Canal on a very sunny 16 February. She was heading for Ellesmere Port where she loaded cargo for Bilbao. Completed by the Damen shipyard in Bergum, her hull had been built by one of Damen's associate companies in eastern Europe, namely Santierul Naval Giurgiu in Romania.

(John Eyres)

It is pleasing to note that sea-going vessels have been encouraged to navigate on the River Rhône in the south of France. Ships sail regularly as far as Lyon (see page 34) and occasionally even further to Chalon on the River Saône. On 22 February, the *Diamant* (LTU, 998gt/85) heads north on the Rhône towards Lyon. She was built at the Ferus Smit shipyard in Westerbroek as *Watum* for Delfzijl-based C Veninga & Zn. In 1995, she was purchased by other Delfzijl owners and, managed by Amasus Shipping, she was renamed *Diamant* at Harlingen in mid-January. She retained this name when acquired by Lithuanian operators in April 2005.

(Annemarie van Oers)

The history of Bibby Line goes back to the early 19th century and it has always been associated with the port of Liverpool. Over the years it has expanded its interests beyond ship owning so it was rather surprising to note its acquisition in 2006 of the coaster *Mira* (CYP, 1854gt/95). As Bibby Line ships were traditionally named after English counties it was appropriate that this new acquisition was also named in this way by being given the name *Hertfordshire*. We see her approaching Aberdeen on 24 February at the end of a voyage from Runcorn. She was built at the Slovenské Lodenice shipyard as *Atair* and was renamed *RMS Atair* for the duration of a charter to RMS between early December 1995 and mid-November 1998. She was renamed *Mira* in February 2006 but in mid-December of that year she transferred to the British flag as *Hertfordshire*.

(David Dodds)

One might expect the River Humber upstream of Hull to be relatively calm. Dispelling that idea, the **Liva Greta** (LVA, 851gt/88) heads up river through the choppy waters of the Humber on 7 March as she makes her way to Flixborough wharf on the River Trent. She departed for Ghent three days later. She exemplifies a popular class of coaster built at the Ferus Smit shipyard and known as the "Ferus Smit 1300" design. Just 60 metres in length and with low air draught, these ships were ideal for upriver trade. Twelve examples were built. Originally named **Varnebank**, this vessel became **Elstar** in 1996 and took her current name in mid-January 2008 when bought by Latvian owners.

(Simon Smith)

The **Rig** (MLT, 2351gt/89) was photographed at Rouen on 25 March. She had arrived from Les Sables d'Olonne four days previously and did not depart until 28 March when she sailed down the River Seine on passage to Harwich. She was built by Estaleiros Navais de Viana do Castelo for Portuguese owners and was initially named **Port Sado**. Later changes of name saw her become **Amrum** in 1993, **Lady Anna** in 1995, **Borneiro** in 2000 and **Rig** in 2005. A useful multi-purpose vessel, she is strengthened for the carriage of heavy cargoes and for navigation in ice, and she has a 153 TEU container capacity.

(Annemarie van Oers)

Having arrived from Pasajes on 25 March, Erwin Strahlmann's *Eider* (ATG, 2452gt/03) was photographed waiting to load a cargo of scrap at the European Metals Recycling wharf at Northam on the River Itchen in Southampton. Photography at this north-facing wharf is never easy. The *Eider* departed on 27 March, bound for Bilbao despite the fact that some movement reports gave her destination as Kiel. The ship had an unusual beginning. An example of the Rhein class from the Slovenské Lodenice yard in Komárno, she had been laid down as long ago as 1998 and, named *Gretchen Müller*, she was one of a group of three coasters whose construction had been delayed because of the closure of the Danube to navigation following the bombing of bridges which in turn put the shipyard in severe financial difficulties. The three ships had been rejected by their original owner and Erwin Strahlmann bought all three, having had one example in his fleet for ten years. The *Eider* was the first of the three, being delivered on 19 February 2003. Strahlmann has ordered several more examples of this class which he rates very highly.

(Colin Drayson)

Now 33 years old, the *Avant* (BHS, 1640gt/75) was photographed on 26 March when she left Hull at the start of a voyage to Borg harbour in Norway, having arrived in the Humber from Lerwick the previous day. One of a surprising number of older tankers to be featured in this volume, she was built at the Nieuwe Noord Nederlandse shipyard in Groningen as *Dutch Glory* for well-known Dutch operator Gebr. Broere. She was sold out of the fleet and renamed *Glory* in mid-January 2001, becoming *West Avant* in mid-October of that same year and *Avant* in 2003.

(Simon Smith)

Having arrived two days previously in ballast from Sharpness, the *Irafoss* (ATG, 1174gt/91) was photographed as she left Boston, Lincolnshire, on 29 March at the start of a voyage to Frederikshavn with a cargo of barley. The ship had an unusual start to her career. The Arminiuswerft shipyard in Bodenwerder on the upper reaches of the River Weser built its first three seagoing ships in the mid-1980s but closed on 31 December 1988. Less than one month later it was reopened by a former manager and was now named Arminius Werke and began to build seagoing ships once again. The second of these was the first of two ordered by Detlef Jensen, of Hamburg, and was named **Hanse Controller**. She sailed downriver to Bremerhaven for fitting out in March 1991 shortly before her owner suffered bankruptcy. Arminius Werke sold her to a Cypriot offshoot of the Hamburg-based Harmstorf shipping company which took delivery at the St Pauli landing stage in Hamburg on 30 April 1991. The coaster had been renamed **Nessand**. Sold on in 1994, she was renamed **Trinket** and became *Irafoss* after purchase by the Eimskip group in 2005.

(David Dixon)

Approaching Aberdeen with a cargo of brine on 1 April is the *Fjordtank* (PAN, 729gt/86). An interesting tanker, she was built at Hakata in Japan by Murkami Hide Zosen K.K. and was originally named **Yamabishi Maru No. 21**. It was in the latter half of 1999 that she left the Far East and was noted at Piraeus between 2 October 1999 and 14 January 2000. During her stay, she was renamed **Triton IV** in late December 1999 and traded in the Mediterranean throughout 2000. Sold at the end of the year to Norwegian owners, she was renamed *Fjordtank* under the Panamanian flag in late January 2001 and passed Cape Finisterre on 18 February on her way to the North Sea and Baltic.

(David Dodds)

The port of Great Yarmouth will soon change in character as a new outer port has been under construction in 2008. It is likely that some of the trade will move to this new port from the long-established wharves on the River Yare. Outward bound to Chatham from the Yare on 5 April is the **Union Mercury** (IOM, 2601gt/01), ex **Estime**-04. Built at the Tille shipyard in Kootstertille, she was in the fleet of Union Transport at the time of the photograph, but later in the year she was purchased by Faversham Ships and renamed **Verity** upon completion of a short charter back to Union Transport until the latter company took delivery of a newbuilding.

(Ashley Hunn)

The hull of the **Flinterbothnia** (NLD, 2474gt/03) was built by Marine Projects Ltd at Gdansk and the ship was completed at the Bodewes shipyard in Hoogezand. We see her discharging a cargo of petroleum coke at the jetty of Anglesey Aluminium at Holyhead. At the time of writing, there are threats that the smelter at Holyhead could be closed which would be a devastating blow to the community where it is the largest employer. The ship departed from Rotterdam on 3 April and was photographed at Holyhead on 7 April, before returning to Rotterdam three days later.

(Dick Richards)

The **Potosi** (ATG, 2506gt/95) leaves the Cumbrian port of Silloth on 8 April bound for Glasgow two days after arrival from Sfax with a cargo of phosphate fertiliser. She is one of several sisterships built for Wessels Reederei at the Slovenské Lodenice shipyard in Komárno on the River Danube. She is an example of the Rostock class from this yard, one of four classes developed specifically for Wessels. This class differed from the others in being designed with container cargoes in mind, each example having a slightly different container capacity. The **Potosi** has a 163 TEU capacity, with 108 in the hold and 55 on deck. Also, the Rostock class ships are fitted with two 12.5-tonne cranes. In August 2009 the port of Silloth, one of the smaller ports in the Associated British Ports group, will commemorate the 150th anniversary of its opening.

(Stephen Wright)

The **Coastal Deniz** (ATG, 3125gt/91) leaves Cardiff on 14 April on the Coastal Container Line service linking the Welsh port to Belfast and Dublin. Coastal Container Line is a wholly-owned subsidiary company of the Mersey Docks & Harbour Board, itself part of the Peel Holdings group. In August 2008, it was announced that the Cardiff service was to close later in the year, increasing fuel costs and the downturn in the Irish economy being blamed. Instead of closing, the service was taken over by Associated British Ports and renamed Cardiff Container Line, this being an operating company of ABP. The **Coastal Wave** (IRL, 2046gt/83) was chartered for the route, with the **Coastal Deniz** remaining on the Liverpool - Ireland link. Built at the Kröger Werft yard at Schacht-Audorf, near Rendsburg, as **Sybille**, she was renamed **Baltic Bridge** for the duration of a charter in 1993 and then **Rhein Merchant** between 1995 and 2000 for a further charter. She took her current name in 2005.

(Bernard McCall)

The Pal Line service between Goole and Swedish ports began in 1977. The following three decades have seen a steady increase in the size of ships used on the service, all of which are chartered vessels. Pal Line is now part of the Transatlantic group and marketed as Trans PalLine UK. The **Trans Agila** (ATG, 2997gt/95) and her sister ships are the largest ever used and represent the biggest ships to use the port of Goole. She was photographed as she passed Hull on her way up river on 22 April. In the distance can be seen two tankers berthed at Saltend jetty.

(Darren B Hillman)

The islands of the West Indies are a popular destination for tourists - and for old coasters from northern Europe. Noted leaving Kingstown (St Vincent) on 24 April is the **Patri** (437gt/57). She was built at the J J Sietas shipyard in Neuenfelde, near Hamburg, as **Barbara** and had the distinction of being the first of the original Sietas standard designs, namely Type A. When built, she had three 2-tonne derricks to serve her three hatches. She became **Pattree** in 1974 when acquired by Ensign Freight Services and she passed through the hands of several British operators before eventually coming into the ownership of Whitbury Shipping Ltd, of Sheerness. Sold to Caribbean owners in August 1985, she was reported to have arrived in Barbados on 13 November 1985. She was renamed **Patri** in 2005.

(Terry Ó Conállain)

The **Sommen** (SWE, 4426gt/83) is of particular note in being the only Chinese-built ship to feature in this volume although we shall see some vessels whose hulls were built in China (page 48). She was built at the Zhonghua shipyard in Shanghai and her engine is also of Far Eastern origin, being a Mitsubishi 2-stroke 6-cylinder diesel of 3900bhp. Operated by Ahlmark Lines, of Karlstad, she is named after a lake in central Sweden as indeed are most of the company's ships. On 1 May, she was photographed at Crown Wharf, Rochester, after discharging a part cargo of timber, the balance having already been discharged in Hull. She is a frequent caller in the Humber and Medway and is used on Ahlmark's liner service from ports on the east coast of Sweden, usually Skelleftehamn, Iggesund and Ala.

(Peter Hutchison)

With the 1400-feet high Rock of Gibraltar dominating the background, the **Atlantis Alvarado** (IOM, 2603gt/04) lies at anchor off Gibraltar on 5 May. She is a typical example of the coastal tankers built at Turkish shipyards during the last decade. Her builders are identified as Gelibolu Gemi Insa Kizaklari Koll. St. at Gelibolu. Although trading initially in the Mediterranean, many of these tankers have been built with the prospect of charter to or purchase by owners in northern Europe and so, like the **Atlantis Alvarado**, have been ice-strengthened. She has ten cargo tanks and, thanks to the fitting of heating coils, is able to carry a wide range of products including heavier grades.

(Martin Penwright)

The Ness at Shaldon, 230 feet high, is a pale comparison to the Rock of Gibraltar, but nevertheless is a pleasing feature dominating the background as the **Celtic Voyager** (BHS, 1957gt/85) leaves Teignmouth on 6 May. An example of the Type 110a standard design from the J J Sietas shipyard, she was built as **Waseberg** for German owners and, along with other examples of this design, came into the fleet of Cardiff-based owners Charles M Willie (Shipping) Ltd in 2005. She had arrived from Greenore two days previously and had loaded a cargo of clay for Barcelona. She topped off her cargo at Fowey before heading south.

(David Walker)

An increasingly important trade over the last twenty years has been the development of fish farms. These have become especially important in areas which offer deep sheltered water close to land. Consequently, the Norwegian fjords and Scottish lochs have become ideal settings. The distribution of feed for the farms has called for enhanced arrangements for distribution and Scottish haulage company Fergusons Transport bought the **Harvest Caroline** (VCT, 712gt/71) for this purpose in May 2006. She is an example of the Europa design from the VEB Elbewerft shipyard at Boizenburg and was originally named **Briland**. She later became **Lundøy** (1973), **Irene** (1979), **Fjord Trader** (1982) and **Fjordbulk** (1984). To release the latter name for a newer vessel, she was briefly renamed **Fjordbulk 2** in 2006 but never traded as such. After two years successful service in western Scotland, she was replaced in the fish feed distribution trade by the **Vermland** which we shall see on page 49. She found further buyers in Norway and, handed over at Hjelmås on 24 October, she was renamed **Straumnes**. We see her at Breasclete (Breascleit in Gaelic) Pier in East Loch Roag which is on the western side of the Isle of Lewis.

(Angus Macleod)

At low water on 12 May the rust streaks on the hull of the **Henny** (NLD, 1241gt/82) are apparent as she lies at Perth on the upper reaches of the navigable River Tay. She departed for Moerdijk at high water later in the evening. She was built at the Peters shipyard in Kampen as **Dependent**, a name that she retained until early January 2001 when she was renamed **Liamare**. Throughout her career thus far, she has remained under the Dutch flag and this continued when she was renamed **Henny** in late April 2004. By the end of the year, the rust streaks had certainly disappeared. She was by then operated by the Flinter Group and her hull had been repainted into that company's smart grey colour.

(David Dodds)

The oldest and arguably the most interesting ship in this year's volume is the **Kumkale** (TUR, 683gt/51). She was launched from the yard of AG Weser, Werk Seebeck, Bremerhaven, on 27 October 1951 and handed over as **Dione** to Swiss owners on 17 November. Managed by well-known German shipping company DDG Hansa, she was the first of three sisterships which were introduced to the company's service to the Iberian peninsula. They had two tanks with a total capacity of 40 m3 for the carriage of wine. On 1 November 1955 all three ships were bought by DDG Hansa and the **Dione** was renamed **Hundseck**. She remained in the fleet until May 1967 when she was bought by French owners and renamed **Baltique**. On 8 January 1970 she grounded on the island of Imroz whilst on passage from Tripoli to Constanta. Although recovered five days later, a storm drove her further ashore on 17 January and she was not salvaged until June 1970. It seems to have been in 1975 that she entered Turkish ownership as **Kumkale**. In 2007 she still had cargo gear but it was thought to be different from the four 3-tonne derricks she originally had. Our photograph shows her in the Bosphorus on 17 May.

(Neil Burns)

There can be little doubt that bridges offer an excellent vantage point for ship photography. However, the photographer must be well prepared to brave the elements. The rewards can be well worthwhile as evidenced by this view of the **Freyja** (MLT, 1665gt/74) as she passed beneath the Forth Bridge on her way to Grangemouth on 21 May. It is remarkable that a tanker of her age has continued to find employment in northern Europe. She was built by J G Hitzler at Lauenburg as **Essberger Pilot**. Renamed **Solvent Explorer** in 1977 and then **Tom Lima** in 1987, she reverted to her original name in 1992. Later name changes saw her become **Hordafor Pilot** in 1997 and finally **Freyja** in 1999.

(David Dodds)

The **RMS Snowlark** (VCT, 1289gt/84) was launched from the Hermann Sürken shipyard in Papenburg on 14 September 1984 and delivered the following month. Originally named **Mosa**, she became **RMS Walsum** when she entered the RMS fleet in 1998. Sold in 2005, she remained on charter to RMS and was renamed **RMS Snowlark**. Our photograph shows her arriving at Teignmouth from Cork on 21 May. She departed on the evening tide, bound for Bendorf with a cargo of ball clay. Her charter to RMS ended in early September 2008 and she was renamed simply **Snowlark**.

(David Walker)

The **Korsika** (ATG, 2997gt/01) makes her way along the Manchester Ship Canal to Ellesmere Port on 21 May, departing for Sagunto two days later. She is yet another example of the ships built in the last decade at the Slovenské Lodenice shipyard in Komárno. Her keel was laid on 23 April 1998 but she was not launched until 29 November 2000 with delivery to owner Siegfried Bojen coming in May 2001. Ships of this design are ideal multipurpose vessels with a 296 TEU container capacity, of which 30 may be refrigerated containers. She is powered by a single 4-stroke 6-cylinder MWM engine of 3467bhp and she has a bow thruster.

(Rosalind Thomas)

As we note elsewhere, a feature of this annual is the number of older tankers which appear despite the ever-stricter regulations which are applied to tankers. On 23 May, the **Bellona** (SWE, 2366gt/65) continues to trade although well over 40 years old and was photographed on the New Waterway on 23 May. She was built in Sweden by Oskarshamns Varv. She was completely rebuilt at Swinoujscie during 1996, having arrived there on 4 October 1995 and not re-entering service until January 1997. Always ice-strengthened for work in the northern Baltic, she emerged with a double hull and was also fitted with a replacement engine. Her original 4-stroke 9-cylinder MAN engine of 1990bhp was replaced by a 4-stroke 6-cylinder MaK engine of 2400bhp which had been made in 1968. One presumes this had been taken from another ship. In December 2008, she sailed west through the English Channel giving her destination as Gibraltar (for orders) and it later transpired that she had been sold to owners in Bulgaria.

(Koos Goudriaan)

The **Kapitan Salih** (TUR, 471grt/54) is a remarkable survivor. She was built at the Westerbroek shipyard of E J Smit & Zoon and was launched as **Alcetas** on 30 May 1954. It was on 20 August 1954 that she was delivered to Nieuwe Kustvaart Mij. NV and taken on charter by KNSM. Sold to Panamanian-flag operators in 1972, she was renamed **Etas**, becoming **Mare 1** in 1976 and then **Sunnybeach** (also rendered as **Sunny Beach**) in 1979. Acquired by Turkish owners and renamed **Kaptan Yasar Akbas** in 1991, she was later removed from Lloyd's Register as her existence was in doubt. In 2001, a sale within Turkey saw her renamed **Afife M,** thus proving her existence. Having been in a collision in late October 2004, she was towed to Iskenderun and arrested. After being refused permission to repair his ship, her owner took the case to court and after a case lasting over two months, the judge found in favour of the owner who then had his ship repaired. She was renamed **Kaptan Salih** in 2006, keeping this name following a reported sale to Syrian owners in 2007. The grey dust would suggest a cargo of cement as she passed Rumeli Kavagi on the Bosphorus on 31 May.

(Simon Smith)

The lines of a coaster built in Hull by the Yorkshire Dry Dock Company Ltd are unmistakable even though the ship is registered in Bratislava and lies at anchor off Istanbul. The **Lider Ceylan** (SVK, 794gt/85) began life as **Hoo Tern** and was bought by her present owners in 2005. It is generally assumed that the "Hoo" ships were owned by Lapthorn but the story is more complex. The **Hoo Tern**, for example, was built for a partnership within the John I Jacobs group and was bareboat chartered to the Lapthorn company by whom she was managed. It was only in 1995 that she was bought by Lapthorns. This photograph was taken in 1 June and although the **Lider Ceylan** is registered in Slovakia she is operated by a company based in Istanbul.

(Simon Smith)

Most of the previous annuals in this series seem to have produced a mystery and this one is no exception. The previous name of this ship is clearly visible. As **Aydin Fatoglu**, she was owned by the Fatoglu family which entered business as a food wholesaler in 1950. In the late 1970s it began wheat flour and wheat bran production and soon saw the need for its own vessel to transport its products. The **Aydin Fatoglu** was built at the Cemalettin Oyar shipyard in Istanbul and was lengthened two years later, resulting in a gross tonnage of 807grt. She was deleted from registers in 2002/3 yet she certainly existed. In late 2007, she was reported to have been named **Elifnaz G** and is seen as such at Pendik, near Istanbul, on 2 June.

(Simon Smith)

The **Jana** (DEU, 1164gt/05), photographed in the lock of the Queen Elizabeth II Oil Dock at Eastham on 4 June, is an unusual caller to a UK port. She is usually to be seen in the Elbe and Kiel Canal areas with occasional visits to the Baltic. This was, however, the first of three visits she made to Eastham; she returned on 13 June and again on 6 November. Owned by Glüsing Transport in Cuxhaven and built locally at the Mützelfeldtwerft yard, she was launched on 14 September 2005 and delivered to her owners on 7 November.

(Rosalind Thomas)

The **Ingunn** (NLD, 2999gt/01) was seen approaching Ipswich and about to pass beneath the A14 road bridge on 14 June. She was built at the Damen shipyard in Foxhol although her hull was constructed by Damen's subsidiary yard in Galati, Romania. Originally named **Merwezoon**, she was completed on 20 April 2001 and was handed over after trials five days later. In 2007 she was sold to Vaagebulk III KS and, having arrived at Sluiskil on 17 June, was renamed **Ingunn** four days later.

(Ed Gray)

Making a welcome change from the plethora of Turkish-built tankers is the **Marte** (ITA, 2708gt/04). She was built at the De Poli shipyard in Pellestrina, an unusual location on a narrow strip of land which separates the Venetian lagoon from the Adriatic Sea, and was launched as **Taygete Star**. Ships are launched into the lagoon. A semi-pressurised and fully-refrigerated gas tanker, her cargo is stored in two tanks with a total capacity of 2940 cubic metres and she is powered by four Yanmar diesel generators supplying power to two directional propulsion units. Although owned in Italy, she is operated by Rotterdam-based Anthony Veder. She was photographed in the St Helen's anchorage to the east of the Isle of Wight, having arrived there from Fawley three days earlier. She remained there until 18 June when she departed for Moerdijk. The photograph was taken during a Solent cruise organised by the Southampton branch of the World Ship Society. Readers are encouraged to take advantage of such cruises organised by WSS branches and other societies such as the Coastal Cruising Association.

(Bernard McCall)

With her original name of **Linda Buck** clearly visible, the **Vitali Kozhin** (ATG, 2295gt/85) has just arrived at Kyle on 15 June and will discharge her cargo of wind turbine blades brought from Esbjerg. She is one of three similar vessels built at the Thyssen Nordseewerke shipyard in Emden for a container service linking Boston, Lincolnshire, to Duisburg on the River Rhine. With bridge forward, they were a distinctive design and were of the maximum size to use the lock at Boston. In February 1993, she grounded off the Dutch coast and was towed to Emden for repair. By early May she was back in service under the name **RMS Britannia** but this was changed to **Britannia** at Boston on 9 July 1993. On 22 July 1996, she reverted to her original name and, after working in the general cargo trades, became **Vitali Kozhin** at Rotterdam on 5 March 2005 prior to taking up service once again from Boston but now connecting the port to Hamburg. In recent years, she has proved an ideal vessel for the carriage of wind farm equipment.

(Alistair MacDonald)

Having arrived in ballast from Poole the previous day, the **Monika** (ATG, 1768gt/77) passes the breakwater at the Hook of Holland on 16 June at the start of a voyage from Rotterdam to New Ross. She was built at the Wartena shipyard of G Bijlsma & Zoon as **Noordland** and completed on 14 October 1977. She was renamed **Stepenitz** in 1988, becoming **Mona Rosa** in 1989 and **Monika** in 2004. When this photograph was taken, she was almost at the end of her career as **Monika**. She arrived at Szczecin on 27 July and was handed over to new owners by whom she was renamed **Christa Kerstin** under the Belize flag.

(Derek & Des Davies)

Celebrating her golden jubilee in 2008 and still going strong is the **Arngast** (DEU, 833gt/58). She was built at the C Lühring shipyard in Brake on the River Weser, her first name appropriately being **Weser** and was delivered on 22 August 1958. In 1964, she was sold and renamed **Baltica**, becoming **Drochtersen** in 1975, **Beta** in 1991 and **Arngast** in 1997. She is still powered by a 4-stroke 6-cylinder Deutz engine, fitted from new, and of a modest 500bhp. This photograph was taken on 17 June at Rendsburg.

(Koos Goudriaan)

The modern profile of the **Tege** (NOR, 1560gt/71) hides the fact that she was built in 1971 and has been modified and refurbished on three occasions since then. She was built by Büsumer Werft as **Atlas Scan** for the Danish heavy-lift specialist Blæsbjerg & Co, of Århus. At that time, she had two heavy-lift derricks of 50 tonnes each. Sold in 1978, she became **Atlantic Sprinter** and then **North Armac** in 1982. Two years later, she was bought by her current owners Chriship AS, from Sortland, Norway, a company whose tradition as shipowners goes back over 150 years. Then given the name **Tege**, the ship has been on a continuous time charter to Tollpost-Globe, her name coming from the two initial letters of her charterer's identity. She is the only ship operated by this express parcel and multimodal freight forwarder and she is employed on a fixed-day tri-weekly liner service from Bodø to Tromsø or Alta via Harstad and Finnsnes. She has been modified and rebuilt on three occasions, the latest in 1998 seeing her given a remodelled higher forecastle, two new 25-tonne cranes and a new bridge structure. Although she now has a top-heavy appearance, the changes have made her more container-friendly and increased her capacity from 77 TEU to 102 TEU. She was photographed as she entered her southern terminal port of Bodø on 19 June. Two months previously, she had collided with the Tromsø bridge in bad weather and had sustained bow damage.

(Uwe Jakob)

The *Erlanda* (VCT, 1999gt/91) passes under the Humber Bridge on 20 June almost at the end of a voyage from Ipswich to Howdendyke; she departed for Amsterdam four days later. She was built as *Scheldeborg* for the Wagenborg company and in June 2003 was acquired by Estonian buyers who gave her her current name and transferred her from the Dutch flag to that of St Vincent & the Grenadines. Her hull was built at the Bijlsma shipyard in Wartena and she was completed at the Westerbroek yard of Ferus Smit.

(Simon Smith)

The *Paula* (ANT, 1945gt/07) was noted entering the Kiel Canal via the old locks at Brunsbüttel at the start of an eastbound transit on 21 June. In the background is an array of vessels awaiting entrance to the Canal. Because of the increasing traffic to and from the Baltic, the Canal will be expanded in coming years. A deeper draught and wider bed will allow the passage of vessels of up to 280 metres in length (currently 235 metres) and 10,5 metres draught (currently 9,8 metres). Moreover, a third large lock will be constructed at Brunsbüttel, adding capacity to the present two large and two small locks. The ship was built by Santierul Naval Giurgiu. Launched on 23 May 2006, she was handed over to her owners on 20 April 2007.

(Oliver Sesemann)

Every inch a Scandinavian coaster, the **Gullfjord** (NOR, 383gt/68) passes southward beneath the 700 metre long Nærøysund Bridge between the Norwegian mainland and Rørvik on the island of Vikna. Her 5-tonne derrick and single hold with a large hatch opening of 21,2m x 5,0m make her an ideal vessel to serve the small ports along the Norwegian coast while her overall length of just 40,2 metres gives her access to berths that newer, larger vessels cannot reach. Built as **Gullfjord**, her hull was constructed by Mandal Slip & Mek Verksted with outfitting by Sig. Iversen Mek Verksted at Flekkefjord. In 1973 she was sold and renamed **Sølvstjernen**, later sales seeing her renamed **Terningen** in December 1982 and **Gullfjell** in December 1993. She reverted to her original name in 1998. Like so many Norwegian coasters, she has seen considerable investment. In 1985, she was lengthened by five metres and the following year her original Callesen engine of 350bhp was replaced by another Callesen of 575bhp. The photograph was taken on 22 June.

(Uwe Jakob)

There is a huge demand for cement in Greece and, indeed, throughout the Mediterranean. To transport this vital commodity, ships of various sizes have been bought and modified whilst purpose-built ships are also used. The **Seacement 1** (GRC, 973gt/68) is an example of the latter and was built as **Ryoyo Maru No. 12** by Tsuneishi Shipbuilding Co Ltd at Numakuma in Japan. The solitary example of a Japanese-built ship in this book, she entered Greek ownership and was renamed in 1993. We see her at Paros on 26 June. She was discharging her cargo into a road vehicle on the quayside, a laborious task that was hindered by a conspicuous shortage of empty vehicles awaiting loading.

(Nigel Jones)

A photograph simply oozing interest. The **Imel Abdena** (ATG, 2541gt/08) had only recently entered service as she made her way westwards along the Kiel Canal on passage from Police, in Poland, to Immingham on 30 June. She is the fourth of the "Jümme" design of coasters to be delivered by the Slovenské Lodenice shipyard in Komárno to Bojen Schiffahrtsbetrieb. Imel Abdena was a tribal leader in the Emden area and it was during his rule that enemies from Hamburg took over Emden in 1433, a rule lasting until 1439. It is interesting to note that the three previous "Jümme" ships in the Bojen fleet were also named after similar tribal leaders. Now united in the fleet, they were enemies in real life! In the background is the preserved **Cap San Diego** (DEU, 9998grt/62) returning passengers from Kiel to Hamburg. She had been in Kiel during Kiel Week when she offered daily voyages from the port to the sailing events in Kiel Bight.

(Oliver Sesemann)

Many coastal cargo ships owned by Norwegian companies are equipped for self-discharge and the **Michelle** (MLT, 3123gt/75), observed southbound in the Baltic on 4 July, is one of the larger examples of such a vessel. She was built by Svendborg Skibsværft as **Amulet** and had a rather different profile from that seen here. Originally she had large angular goalpost masts fore and aft to each of which was fitted a 6-tonne derrick. She also had a rail-mounted 5-tonne gantry crane on deck. Following sale in 1994 to Norwegian owner R G Hagland AS, this gear was removed and she now carries a Caterpillar 245 excavator/grab. In 1991 she had been given a new engine, this being a powerful 4-stroke 12-cylinder Wärtsilä 12V25F engine of 3084bhp.

(Jimmy Christie)

The **Pommern** (ATG, 2061gt/94) was launched at the Slovenské Lodenice shipyard on 30 October 1994 and handed over to owners Wessels Reederei two months later. Typical of the builder's output in the mid-1990s, she is a handy multi-purpose vessel, is ice-strengthened, and is powered by a 4-stroke 6-cylinder Deutz engine of 1530bhp. She was photographed as she departed from Sharpness and entered the Severn estuary on 4 July at the start of a voyage to Waterford with a cargo of organic wheat bran pellets.

(Mike Nash)

The **Steenborg** (DEU, 718gt/67) was launched from the Friedrich Krupp shipyard, later to become Ruhrorter Schiffswerft, in Duisburg on 29 April 1967 and delivered on 21 October of that year. She traded as **Berta Morgenroth** until 1981 when she was sold and renamed **Steenborg**. Noted passing Warnemünde on 8 July, this photograph clearly shows the different dimensions of her hatches with No. 1 hatch being 15,59 metres long and No. 2 hatch being only 8,39 metres. Until a few years ago, she was equipped with three 3-tonne derricks. Roland Mehl is a Bremen-based flour miller with another mill at Büsum to which wheat is carried from various parts of Schleswig-Holstein by the **Steenborg**.

(Simon Smith)

The identity of this vessel has posed some problems. A transliteration of her Cyrillic name suggests that she is named **Princessa Arktiki** or, to be more exact **Printsessa Arktiki** which reflects the pronunciation of the Cyrillic letters. The name on her bridge board, however, and that used in official registers and lists is **Arctic Princess**. Classed as a refrigerated cargo ship of 1966gt, she was built as a refrigerated cargo ship in 1977 by Brattvåg Skippsinnredning as **Utstraum** for Norwegian owners. Sold within Norway in 1985, she was renamed **Sea Rose** and was rebuilt the following year, Lloyd's Register noting that she had become a fish factory ship. Following a further sale within Norway, she became **Arctic Princess** in 1988. Lloyd's Register at the time noted that it was in 1988 that she was converted to a fish factory ship but she was sold to Russian owners, based in Murmansk, in the mid-1990s and was once again classed as a refrigerated cargo ship. With the current register noting that she has a single crane rather than the four derricks seen clearly in the photograph taken at IJmuiden on 8 July, her name and exact configuration have clearly posed problems over the years.

(Kevin Jones)

Her present identity, rather roughly painted on her bow, may not provide many clues about the history of this coaster but the raised letters of her original name, clearly visible, certainly do tell us what we need to know. Of 1599gt, she was built in 1969 at the Ivan Dimitrov shipyard in Rousse, Bulgaria, as **Trojan** and was one of a class of fourteen similar ships sometimes known as the Sopot type, after the name of the lead ship. Sold out of Bulgarian ownership in 1997, she was renamed **Wind II**, later becoming **Vika** (2000), **Ira** (2002), and **Gull** (2005). Most sources suggest that she was renamed **Samy** in 2007 but there is photographic evidence that she had this name in 2005. She was used in the 2006 thriller film "Cargo". Photographed at Barcelona on 11 July where she had been laid up for over three years, she retains her original two 5-tonne cranes.

(Trevor Jones)

31

On the Haringvliet south-west of Rotterdam is the attractive small town of Hellevoetsluis and it is here that the **Merel-V** (NLD, 2438gt/05) is registered. Like so many Dutch-built coasters in this book, two yards were involved in her construction. The "Leda" shipyard in Korcula, Croatia, built her hull and she was completed at the Peters shipyard in Kampen. Owned by Henk Veltman, she is named after his daughter. Although the V suffix of the ship's name comes from the family's surname, it is especially appropriate as the ship is the fifth in the series of nine ships known as Saimaamax from the Peters yard. These ships have been designed to fit the dimensions of the locks on the Saimaa Canal in Finland and carry the maximum amount of cargo, estimated at 200 tonnes more than other ships of a similar length. Her engine is a 4-stroke 12-cylinder Caterpillar of 1700bhp. Heading for the Ghent Canal, she is seen passing Vlissingen on 17 June.

(Martin Wright)

It was in 1899 that Peter Madsen Schmidt bought his first ship. The Schmidt family has continued to own one or occasionally two ships since that time and the **Uno** (DIS, 1473gt/86) is the fifth to have carried that name and is owned by Peter Rasmus Schmidt and Erik Petersen Schmidt, the two great-grandsons of Peter Madsen Schmidt. Based near the city of Fredericia, the family has permission to use the city's shield on the bow of ships in the fleet and the **Uno** is the only coaster presently using Fredericia as her port of registry. She was built at the Sliedrecht shipyard of J H van Eijk & Zonen. Launched on 28 May 1986, she was delivered to her original German owner as **Elke** on 17 October 1986. She was purchased by the Schmidt brothers on 3 January 2003 and was handed over one week later at Vlaardingen. The next generation in the family has not been involved in a seagoing career so it is likely that this, the twelfth vessel to have been owned by the family, will be the last. We see her passing through the English Channel on 19 July, on passage from Duisburg to Bilbao.

(Dominic McCall)

A glance at the hull of the **Doris K** (DNK, 1022gt/82) reveals immediately that she has had recent surgery. This coaster was built at the Kötter Werft shipyard in Haren/Ems. Launched in October 1982, she was handed over as **Gerhard Prahm** to owners Hammann & Prahm, of Wischhafen, on 24 November. Between late December 1992 and mid-September 1996, she was chartered by RMS and was renamed **RMS Bavaria**, reverting to her original identity at the end of the charter. In 2002 she was sold to Karl Meyer also based in Wischhafen and was renamed **Seeland** in early June. Early in 2008 she was sold to Danish buyers and in April arrived at Thyborøn for conversion to a suction dredger to trade as **Doris K**. This work had been completed by early June. We see her at the Danish port of Lemvig on 23 July.

(Flemming Nees)

The year 2008 saw a change in the type of vessel importing timber to Wisbech on the River Nene. A decade ago, it was Russian STK type ships that were used but these later gave way to the Ladoga classes. Now these too have been superceded and the cargoes are brought by ships of the more modern "Vyg" design. The **Tulos** (RUS, 1596gt/95) was built at the Arminius Werke shipyard at Bodenwerder on the upper reaches of the River Weser and was handed over to owners White Sea - Onega Shipping Company in January 1995. She was noted at Wisbech on 24 July.

(Darren Green)

It seems quite remarkable that a ship built over half a century ago should return to service after over a decade laid up but that has been the fortune of the **Baltic Breeze 1** (PAN, 397gt/52). She was built at the C Lühring shipyard in Brake and launched on 21 August 1952 as **Westfjord**, being handed over to her Swedish owners in September of that year. She was lengthened by 4,4 metres in 1954. Her first change of identity came in 1969 when she was renamed **Hamnfjord** and she would subsequently become **Vänerfjord** (1976), **Sea Glory I** (1991), **New Sea** (1992), and **Baltic Breeze** (early March 1997). It was under this name that she arrived at Ronnebyhamn, north of Stockholm, during August 1997. There were reports that she had been sold on at least one occasion over the following ten years but she remained at Ronnebyhamn. This sale became a reality in late 2007 and she returned to service in early 2008. Our photograph shows her at Århus on 24 July.

(Bent Mikkelsen)

Our third vessel noted on 24 July is the **Fri Star** (BHS, 1499gt/81), seen at the inland port of Lyon on the River Rhône after arrival from Taranto. The ship was built at the Hugo Peters shipyard in Wewelsfleth and launched as **Pax** on 27 May 1981. Handed over to German owners the following month, she was sold without change of name to Svendborg-based Danish operators in 1990. She became **Fri Star** after entering the fleet of Kopervik Ship Management in August 2001. The port of Lyon is 330 kilometres (just over 200 miles) from the sea at Marseilles and is a rapidly-expanding industrial area handling some 10 million tonnes of goods annually. In addition to riverside wharves there are four dock basins and the **Fri Star** is seen at one of the six covered berths in the port.

(Annemarie van Oers)

Cruises to Baltic ports have become very popular in recent years. For ship enthusiasts, these can sometimes offer a sail along the Kiel Canal - but potential passengers are advised to check beforehand whether this passage is made in daylight hours. In addition to the passing ships, there is almost certain to be at least one ship tied up at the Kreishafen in Rendsburg. On 25 July, our photographer has a fine view of the **Barentszzee** (NLD, 1045gt/73), ex **Gersom**-95, **Realta**-87, which seems to have almost completed discharge of her cargo. Launched from the Werftunion shipyard in Emden on 12 October 1973, she was delivered two months later.

(Teun Put)

The shipyard at Appledore has a long and proud history but in recent years has faced great uncertainty. In June 2007, Babcock Marine took over Devonport Royal Dockyard in Plymouth from DML, a company which also owned the shipyard at Appledore and pledged to continue the latter town's long history of shipbuilding. The most recent vessel built has been a 96-metre long "superyacht" for an unidentified billionnaire. Known only as "Project 55", this work has been shrouded in secrecy. On 31 July, the **RMS Vindava** (BLZ, 1307gt/89), ex **RMS Rahm**-07, **Henning-S**-05, brought a deck cargo of steel fittings for this yacht from Bremen. We see her leaving Appledore on 1 August, bound for Belfast to discharge her main cargo of animal feed. The coaster was built at the Hermann Sürken shipyard in Papenburg.

(Bernard McCall)

There is so much to comment on in this photograph that the caption could take its own page. We start with the coaster. The **Frelon** (MLT, 1354gt/91) was built at the Erlenbach/Main shipyard of Bayerische Schiffbauges. mbH vom A Schellenberger and was the first newbuilding to be ordered by Frank Dahl. She was of a revolutionary design, being powered by water jets rather than conventional propeller and rudder. This system enabled her to load 1180 tonnes of cargo on a draught of only 2,5 metres. Launched as **Orade** on 14 December 1990, there were initial problems and the ship was not handed over until 2 April 1991. She entered service on charter to Seacon as **Sea Orade**. The charter ended in 1998 and during that year her water jets were replaced by twin propellers and a rudder. She was sold and renamed **Frelon** in mid-2007. We see her on the River Rhône on 2 August. She had loaded 1600 tonnes of scrap at Salaise and was bound for Genoa. She is passing the nuclear power station at Cruas, near Montélimar. Further details of the ship and the setting will be published in *Coastal Shipping* magazine during 2009.

(Annemarie van Oers)

The various wharves on the River Trent continue to handle a significant number of coasters with a wide variety of cargoes. On 10 August the **Sea Ruby** (CYM, 1382gt/92) was photographed as she discharged a cargo of animal feed at Flixborough Wharf. She departed the next day, arriving at Boston, Lincolnshire on 12 August. She is one of the last group of coasters to have been built for operation by the Lapthorn company by the Yorkshire Drydock Co Ltd. Initially named **Hoo Larch**, she was bareboat chartered to R Lapthorn & Co Ltd from John I Jacobs plc and entered Lapthorn ownership in 1995. She was one of three Lapthorn vessels sold in 2002 to BUE Marine Ltd for a contract in the Caspian Sea. Preparation for this work was protracted and they were unable to reach the Caspian Sea before the ending of the navigation period on the Russian waterways so all three were time chartered back to Lapthorn. The Caspian contract then was cancelled and management of the ships was taken over by Union Transport, the **Hoo Larch** being renamed **Union Ruby**. In 2004, she was sold to Boddington Shipping Ltd and Firth Shipping Ltd, with management in the hands of Torbulk Ltd; she was renamed **Sea Ruby**.

(David H Smith)

Having arrived at Fos from Valencia two days previously, the ***Paganini*** (ATG, 2971/07) is awaiting departure on 10 August after loading a cargo at the huge Sollac steel works, part of which forms the backdrop to the photograph. The ship is the third in a series of ten ships being built for Wessels Reederi and was built at the Rousse shipyard in Bulgaria. It is reported that later ships in the series will be built at the Slovenské Lodenice shipyard. Although the ***Paganini*** was launched on 17 April 2007, her keel had been laid down as long ago as 25 June 1998. She was christened in Hamburg on 5 October 2007 and proceeded to load 4000 tonnes of potash for Piombino on her maiden commercial voyage. She will trade for the K&S Group, one of the world's leading suppliers of speciality and standard fertilisers. Following the signing of new long-term freight contracts with Mediterranean buyers, Kali-Transport, a subsidiary of K&S, has partly financed ten newbuildings including the ***Paganini***.

(John P Robinson)

The ***Carrier*** (ATG, 1584gt/85) is one of six similar coasters built by Husumer Schiffswerft inh Gebr Kröger, two of these being bought by Erwin Strahlmann. She was launched on 27 September 1985 and delivered as ***Inga*** to her first owner, Jan-Peter Lüdtke, on 25 October. German sources report that she was modified in 1995 with her draught being increased from 3,64 metres to 4,21 metres resulting in her deadweight changing from 1900dwt to 2378dwt. Modifications were also made to her bow as part of the work. She was acquired by Erwin Strahlmann and renamed ***Carrier*** in March 2002. We see her outward bound in the River Trent on 14 August at the start of a voyage from Flixborough to Cagliari.

(Roy Cressey)

It has been claimed that the advent of cheap flights has dealt a fatal blow to some ferry links within Europe. That is perhaps only part of the reason, but there is no doubt that ferry links have been much reduced in the last decade. One sad loss in 2008 was the link between Newcastle and Norway which offered a splendid cruise along the Norwegian coast between Stavanger and Bergen, and gave ship enthusiasts some excellent views of passing ships. Several ships could always be seen in the Haugesund area and on 17 August, the **Baltic Sky** (DMA, 2061gt/80) was noted there. She is a sistership of the **Cailin** (page 52), the whole class numbering seven ships. Built at the Rauma-Repola shipyard in Uusikaupunki, she was initially named **Repola** and was built to the builders' own account. After being laid up for much of 1983, she was sold in 1984 and renamed **Ann Ragne**. Later changes of name have seen her become **Ann-Mari** (1986), **Svarte** (1990), **Borre af Simrishamn** (1991), **Borre** (1997), **Bolero** (2000), **Marlen** (January 2005) and **Baltic Sky** (August 2005).

(Martin Penwright)

On 22 August the **Bawa I** (MLT, 335gt/72) enters the Grand Harbour at Valletta. She was built as an effluent tanker and traded as **Minol 14** until 1981. She was constructed by Stocznia Rzeczna at Wroclaw and fitted with a 4-stroke 6-cylinder Sulzer engine of a modest 440bhp which was, no doubt, sufficient for her intended use within harbours and estuaries. It is reported that she was converted to a bunkering tanker in 2006.

(Roger Musselwhite)

The future of the port of Whitstable, owned by the local council, is uncertain. After a brief revival in the import of timber a few years ago, the sole cargo handled has been the import of stone with only about three ships per month calling at the port. Most of the stone is brought by Union Transport ships from northern France or from the Isle of Grain but there are also occasional cargoes from Methil on the Firth of Forth and it is these that tend to bring some variety to Whitstable's shipping scene. On 30 August, the **Bravery** (NLD, 1552gt/04) arrived from Methil. She was the third in a series of four coasters known as the Damen Combi Coaster 1700 design and was built at the Damen shipyard in Bergum. Towed from the yard to Harlingen on 4 October 2004, she underwent trials the next day and was handed over to owners Amasus Shipping BV, of Delfzijl, on 8 October. These vessels were designed for the transport of steel from the Ruhr region to the UK.

(Derek Weatherall)

As the years go by, it is increasingly difficult to include a vessel that was built in a UK shipyard. The **Karim** (KHM, 3658gt/75) appears initially to be a rather unlikely candidate but she was built by Appledore Shipbuilders and was one of two sistership from this yard. Originally named **Risnes**, she became **Selnes** in 2004 and **Wilson Muuga** in 2004. On 19 December 2006 she grounded in bad weather off the coast of Iceland having just commenced a voyage from Grundartangi to Murmansk. A Danish coastguard vessel was in the area and sadly one member of its crew was lost following the capsize of a rescue boat which had been launched to provide assistance. A helicopter rescued the 12-man crew of the **Wilson Muuga** which was soon settled as a constructive total loss. No salvage attempt could be made for almost four months but the ship was towed off the reef and taken to Hafnarfjördur. Despite extensive damage, she was partially repaired and sold to Lebanese buyers by whom she was renamed **Karim**. She sailed to Tripoli, arriving on 23 June, and repairs continued. She eventually returned to service on 1 December 2007. It seems astonishing that so much time and money was spent on a vessel over 30 years old. We see her here at Ipswich on 31 August.

(David Eeles)

It is unusual for a coaster built in Spain to be acquired by owners in Scandinavia but the **Vestland** (PAN, 1023gt/84) is an example of just such a vessel. She was built at the shipyard of José Valiña Lavandeira in La Coruña. In November 1994 she was sold to Norwegian owners and renamed **Sevald**. She went to a shipyard in Trondheim to be refurbished and then in April of the following year she was sold again, this time staying in Norway with her new owners being based in Måløy. Renamed **Vestland** she was then fitted with self-discharge equipment. We see her at the Danish port of Lemvig on 3 September.

(Flemming Nees)

Such is the demand for the carriage of cement in bulk that several conventional coasters have been converted to dedicated cement carriers in recent years. The **Cemsea** (CYP, 2827gt/94) is a product of the Ferus Smit shipyard in Westerbroek and traded for the Flinter Group as **Flinterland** for ten years. She was sold and converted to a cement carrier at Szczecin in Spring 2004. Our photograph shows her off Cape Wrath on the morning of 5 September. She was on passage to Nuuk in Greenland.

(Richard Jones)

On 13 September, the **Bremer Elena** (GIB, 3172gt/07) makes her way through the rural landscape of the Kiel Canal whilst on passage from the Swedish ports of Solvesborg and Skutskär to Zeebrugge. Owned by Rörd Braren, of Kollmar, a small village on the River Elbe downstream from Hamburg, she is one of a fleet of ships which have been designed to be environmentally friendly with low fuel consumption and low emissions. This offers a big advantage for Braren ships in view of fluctuating oil prices and low-sulphur fuel regulations which are due to be introduced in the Baltic in the near future. The hull of the **Bremer Elena** was built by Santierul Naval S. A. Giurgiu and completed at the Bodewes yard in Hoogezand. She is one of 21 vessels of her type which differ mainly with regard to cargo gear.

(Oliver Sesemann)

After several years on the Feederlink container service linking Rotterdam and Europoort to ports on the east coast of England, the **Hajo** (ATG, 3818gt/91) came off this charter at the end of March 2008 and began to work in the general cargo trades, making visits to the Mediterranean and Black Sea. On 13 September, however, she arrived at Hull with a cargo of steel from Emden. This photograph provides ample evidence that she was a large vessel to enter Albert Dock in Hull, and the photographer notes that it took her a long time to be warped around the knuckle to enter the lock. An example of the Type 129 standard design from J J Sietas, she was launched on 12 December 1990 and delivered as **Nancop** in January 1991. Her litany of subsequent names reveals her charterers. She was renamed **City of Valletta** in May 1991, later becoming **Nincop** (April 1992), **Norasia Alexandria** (mid-1993), **Nincop** (March 1995), **OPDR Tejo** (July 1995), **Nincop** (January 1999), **Portlink Sprinter** (June 2002) and **Hajo** (March 2004).

(Roy Cressey)

The Wessels family is one of the oldest seafaring families in the German town of Haren/Ems. In the 1960s, Kapitän Gerhard Wessels joined the increasing trend away from captain/owners in favour of land-based ship ownership as coasters became bigger and more expensive to cope with increasing containerisation. Wessels was at the forefront of innovative ship design and construction. In the early 1990s he quickly realised the potential for building ships at yards in eastern Europe where costs would be less and since that time he has had various classes of ships built in these countries. The **Wotan** (ATG, 2997gt/96) was built by the Slovenské Lodenice yard in Komárno and is an example of the Schelde class built for one of Wessels' subsidiary companies. We see her arriving at Runcorn Dock on 14 September. She departed for Antwerp two days later.

(Rosalind Thomas)

We can say for certain that it is the first occasion that we have featured an Albanian port in one of our annuals. The port is Saranda, serving a city that is rapidly becoming the southern gateway for tourists entering Albania. There are frequent ferry services from Corfu. The **Edro II** (SLE, 1798gt/68) has had a series of identities in recent years and has been found wanting during port state control inspections in several countries. She began life as **Konstantin Shestakov**, built by the Vyborg shipyard for the Russian state merchant fleet and is notable as being the first example of a class of twenty ships known as the "Soviet Warrior" ("Sovietskiy Voin") class, after the second in the series. Sold out of Russian ownership in 1998, she was renamed **Miso** then becoming **Cirrus** in 2002, **Kairos** in 2003, **Ata Atun** in 2007 and **Edro II** in February 2008. She retains her two 8-tonne cranes from her Russian days.

(Nigel Jones)

Our fourth and final RMS coaster is the **RMS Wedau** (ATG, 1556gt/85). Another product of the Hugo Peters shipyard in Wewelsfleth, she was launched on 9 March 1985 and was completed in April. Built as **Dania Carina**, she was renamed **Moldavia** in 1996 and **RMS Wedau** in 2003. On a sunny 19 September she arrives at Teignmouth from Sharpness on the morning tide and she departed on the evening tide of the same day, bound for Bendorf with a cargo of ball clay just like her erstwhile fleetmate on page 20.

(Ken Loak)

Seen in gentle evening sunlight at Sharpness on 20 September, the **Maya** (ATG, 2318gt/82) was discharging a cargo of ammonium nitrate fertiliser that she had brought from Immingham. German shipyards built a large number of low air draught coasters in the 1980s and the names of yards such as J J Sietas and Hugo Peters will be very familiar to followers of coastal vessels. The MAN/GHH Sterkrade yard, also known as Rheinwerft Walsum, on the River Rhine near Duisburg was a much smaller yard and was better known for building barges. In the early 1980s, however, it built three coasters for the innovative Wessels company, the final one being the **Lena Wessels**. From a fairly unusual start, the coaster has had an interesting career. In December 1984, when on charter to RMS, she was driven aground by heavy winds and all crew were taken off by helicopter with the exception of her Master, Kapitän Manfred Draxl. Thanks to his skill, the ship was saved and he became a shipowner himself the following year. In 1987, the **Lena Wessels** was sold to Civil & Marine and converted to a self-discharging bulk carrier named **Cambrook**. On 30 July 2001, she was laid up in the River Fal. She departed on 21 November, bound for Tallinn where she was handed over to Estonian owners on 3 December. Renamed **Maya**, she was extensively refurbished prior to re-entry into service.

(Cedric Catt)

Over the last two decades, the Piraeus-based Vassilios Shipping Company has built up an interesting fleet of small second-hand tankers, mostly of north European or Japanese origin. They trade almost exclusively in the Mediterranean although it is certainly not unknown for them to venture back to northern Europe on occasions. On 26 September, the **Vassilios XV** (GRC, 753gt/65) is seen at Argostoli in Greece. The tanker has an interesting history. She was launched at the Elmshorn yard of D W Kremer Sohn on 21 September 1964 and, named **Indio**, handed over to owner Atlantic Rhederei F & W Joch on 8 February 1965. Construction had begun for the yard's own account as it had no other orders and Atlantic bought the ship prior to launching. In February 1973 the **Indio** was sold to the Swedish Navy and, following handover on 2 March, was renamed **HMS Braennaren** with the pennant number A228. After two decades in naval service, she was acquired by Vassilios and renamed **Vassilios XV**. She proved to be Atlantic's last newbuilding at the Kremer yard which could not build the bigger ships required by Atlantic. Subsequent tankers were built at the Lindenau yard in Kiel.

(Peter Hobday)

There can be few better places for bunkering in the UK than Falmouth. The larger vessels anchor in Falmouth Bay but others come into Carrick Roads. Recent years have seen various tankers used for supplying bunkers and in Autumn 2008, the **Vadero Highlander** (NIS, 1300gt/03) was being used for this work. She was photographed on 28 September. Built at the Tersanesi shipyard in Tuzla on the outskirts of Istanbul, she was launched as **Kerem D** but was soon renamed **Montipora** and in June 2004 became **Crescent Highlander**. When Crescent Marine Services was subsumed within the Clipper Group, she became **Clipper Highlander** in August 2006. She took her current name in late February 2008.

(David Fletcher)

The private wharf at Burton-upon-Stather on the River Trent, more accurately known as King's Ferry Wharf, has had several owners over the last decade and has fallen into disuse on more than one occasion. Trade was revived during March 2008 with the import of bagged cement from Pula and the second vessel to deliver such a cargo was the much-renamed **Pardi** (PAN, 1939gt/82) which arrived on 2 October. Starting her career as **Katja**, a Type 110 coaster from the Sietas yard, she became **Birte Wehr** (1990), **Humber Star** (1995), **Birte Wehr** (January 1999), **Nandia** (July 1999), **Miktat N** (2004) and then **Pardi** in July 2008.

(Andrew Kitchen)

Even the use of hulls built in eastern Europe was unable to save the Pattje shipyard on the Winschoterdiep in northern Holland which closed in 2001. The hull of the **Merit** (GIB, 2301gt/00) was built by Daewoo-Mangalia Heavy Industries in Mangalia and was towed to Holland, along with that of sistership **Nikar G**, by the tug **Towing Diamond**. Most sources say that the ship was completed at the Pattje shipyard in Waterhuizen but this is not correct; she was, in fact, completed at Eemshaven. She was photographed at anchor off Wick on 3 October, awaiting better weather to sail through the Pentland Firth to Killybegs in Ireland with a cargo of wind farm equipment.

(Richard Jones)

The **Polla Rose** (402gt/71), ex **Geminus**-08, **Zuiderzee**-85, **Bornrif**-83, **Veritas**-79, **Dolfijn**-75, has an interesting history. She is the last example of a "Denmark Trader", a vessel designed and built to trade between Dutch ports and Denmark. As much of this voyage would be close to land, the ships had two deadweight tonnages with 530dwt being available on voyages up to 50 miles offshore but 730dwt for voyages on inland waterways. In 2003 she was bought for trade on the Mersey and Manchester Ship Canal but failed to find regular use. In early 2008 she was sold to Thames Shipping, a subsidiary of Euromix, and was renamed **Polla Rose**. On 5 May she was towed away from the Manchester Ship Canal to Acorn Shipyard at Rochester where she was upgraded for her new role which was to carry aggregate from Fingringhoe on the River Colne downstream from Colchester to Mohawk Wharf on the River Thames. This cargo would be used in the construction of buildings for the 2012 Olympics. We see her at Mohawk Wharf on 8 October.

(David Eeles)

On 11 October, an unseasonably hot day, the **Ashley** (NLD, 2056gt/00) was photographed in the River Crouch as she made her way to the wharf which is generally called Creeksea but should more accurately be described as Wallasea Island. Yet another coaster to have been built in two shipyards, her hull was fabricated by Ceskoslovenska Plavba Labska at Decin and she was completed at the Peters yard in Kampen. She took her current name in July 2007 after trading as **Hydra** since her entry into service.

(Stuart Emery)

As we reported in the 2007 "annual", the Lapthorn fleet was taken over by Coastal Bulk Shipping Ltd which worked hard to upgrade the ships and market them as ideal vessels for short sea bulk trades. Just when all seemed to be going well for the new company and its ships, it found itself in a position where it had to cease trading on 18 December 2008. The notorious "credit crunch" was partly responsible as was the failure of some customers to fulfil contracts. Underlying this, though, is a feeling that the ships were having to compete on unequal terms with road haulage. The **Curlew** (794gt/86) arrives at Perth on 13 October. Like the **Lider Ceylan** (page 22), she was built by the Yorkshire Dry Dock Co Ltd in Hull for a company within the John I Jacobs group and, named **Hoocrest**, she was chartered to the Lapthorn company. It was not until 1995 that she entered Lapthorn ownership. She was renamed **Curlew** in early 2007 after being taken over by Coastal Bulk Shipping.

(Richard Jones)

Autumn sunlight illuminates the **Coral Sea** (NLD, 2137gt/00) as she heads north through the Sound of Mull on 15 October. She was returning to Esbjerg from Glasgow having delivered a cargo of wind farm equipment. She made several deliveries of these cargoes during 2008. She was built at the Tille shipyard in Kootstertille as **Deo Volente** for the Hartman family in Urk. In late 2005 she was replaced by a newer and larger vessel of the same name and on 22 December she was sold to a company associated with another member of the Hartman family, being renamed **Coral Sea**.

(Charlie McCurdy)

Over the last decade, there are three fleets which have started to dominate coastal trade in northern Europe. These are the fleets of Arklow Shipping in Ireland, the Wilson Group in Norway, and Erwin Strahlmann in Germany. In 2007/8, several newbuildings were added to the Strahlmann fleet and older vessels were sold. Remaining in service for the company was the **Elbetor** (ATG, 2351gt/90), built for Portuguese owners as **Port Faro** at the shipyard in Viana do Castelo. Later changes of name saw her become **Baltrum** in 1993, **Lada Clara** in 1995 and **Elbetor** in 2005. Here we see her at Great Yarmouth on 21 October. She had arrived from Gunness and sailed later that day for Les Sables d'Olonne in western France.

(David Brady)

Readers will obviously have noticed the ever-increasing number of coasters whose hulls are built cheaply in eastern Europe and then towed to a yard in north-west Europe for completion. We now find that hulls are being built in Chinese yards and delivered on barges from the Far East. On 23 October, our photographer was on hand to record the arrival in the New Waterway of four coasters of the Bijlsma Trader design. Only one carried a name and that was **Priscilla**. Another was later noted at the Dockside Shipyard in IJsselmonde and she was named **Jade**. At the time of writing, no names are known for the other two vessels but their IMO numbers are 9411745 and 9411757.

(Koos Goudriaan)

The stretch of water known as The Swale separates the Isle of Sheppey from "mainland" Kent. Its southern bank offers excellent vantage points for taking photographs of ships heading to or from Ridham Dock and Grovehurst Jetty. Clearly visible in this photograph, taken on 28 October, is the Sheppey Crossing which was opened on 3 July 2006 and is the first fixed bridge across The Swale. The rather unimaginative name of the bridge was selected as a result of a local competition. About to pass beneath the bridge is the **Olga** (NLD, 2561gt/94) whose distinctive scarlet hull identifies her as part of the Wijnne & Barends fleet. She was built at the Niestern Sander shipyard in Delfzijl and was the fourth of seven sistership built at the yard for Wijnne & Barends between 1991 and 1996.

(Kevin Bassett)

As noted on page 18, the **Harvest Caroline** was replaced by the **Vermland** (NOR, 608gt/70) for the distribution of feed to the fish farms on the west coast of Scotland. Although older than the **Harvest Caroline**, she has had some significant modifications. She was built at the Lindstøl shipyard in Risør as **Gerd Gaustadnes** and was initially used for the transport of LECA. Following the bankruptcy of her original owners in 1973, she was sold and renamed **Vermland**. She was lengthened in 1979. She entered the fish farm trade when bought by Trondheim-based owners in 1993 and she was fitted with a new engine two years later. In 2004, she was once again modernised and was equipped for handling bulk cargoes of pellets with pneumatic discharge and also big bags of pellets to be discharged by crane. Our photograph shows her passing Kyle for the first time on 31 October.

(Alistair MacDonald)

One can never be certain which ships will appear in photographs submitted for possible inclusion in our annuals. The **Anina** (JAM, 885gt/70) is certainly one of the most remarkable in 2008. She was seen at anchor off St George's Harbour, Grenada, on 31 October. The West Indies continues to be the home of older conventional coasters such as the **Patri** (page 16) but here we have a very different kind of coaster. She is one of a class of container feeder ships built by VEB Elbewerft at Boizenburg for the state-operated fleet of the German Democratic Republic (East Germany) and was originally named **Trinwillershagen**. From March 1992, she was laid up at Zaandam but had been renamed **Anina** by early 1993 and she was soon trading along the coast of South Africa. There she remained for three years and then by early summer she was in the West Indies where she has remained.

(Charlie McCurdy)

The **Torpo** (BHS, 1986gt/90) appeared in *Coasters 2007* and we try to avoid repetition, especially in consecutive years, unless there is a reason. In fact there are two reasons for taking another look at this coaster. The first is a technical one. By the date of this photograph, 1 November 2008, she had lost the prominent 35-tonne crane which she possessed in 2007. The second reason is aesthetic. The still waters of Loch Linnhe and the brooding Morvern hills in the background combine to make this a photograph well worth inclusion. The ship has just left Corpach, near Fort William, at the start of a voyage to Follafoss in Norway. The ship was built at the Bodewes shipyard in Hoogezand and was completed in June 1990.

(Mike Hemming)

In previous annuals, we have commented on the growth in exports of round timber from Scottish forests which have resulted in a revival of trade at several previously-disused wharves and jetties. Two ships owned by Troon-based Taylor and Taylor have been busy in this trade for several years, the second one to be added to the fleet being the **Red Duchess** (1285gt/69). Built by Scheepswerf Hoogezand at Bergum, this ship was launched as **Gertien Bos** but entered service as **Valdes** when on charter. In 1973, a charter to Bell Lines saw her become **Bell Cavalier**, reverting to **Valdes** in 1974 and to **Bell Cavalier** in 1975. She retained this name until 1978 when she was renamed **Minitrans**. The next change of identity saw her renamed **Aasland** in 1986 and finally **Red Duchess** in 2005. Late in 2008, she was bought by Coast Lines Shipping Ltd who plan to use her more widely than solely in the timber trade. Indeed shortly after purchase she delivered a cargo of stone to Plymouth and it was when she was heading west to Waterford that she sought shelter in Mount's Bay in early November. She eventually berthed at Newlyn and became the first coaster to do so for several years and flew the Cornish flag as a courtesy during her stay. Photographed on 11 November, it is the unusual location which justifies the inclusion of a ship that appeared in Coasters 2006.

(Geoff Hoather)

We stay in Cornwall and on a pleasantly sunny 1 December, the **Oostzee** (LVA, 815gt/78) approaches Duchy Wharf, Falmouth, at the end of a voyage from Poland. She was bringing steel products and fittings for the refit of the Royal Fleet Auxiliary vessel **Argus** which would be undertaken at the Falmouth shipyard in early 2009. An attractive coaster, she was built at the van Goor shipyard in Monnickendam for Dutch owners as **Almenum**. In 1991, she was replaced by another vessel of the same name and she was renamed **Almenum 1**, arriving thus at Krimpen aan den Lek on 7 January 1992. By early March, she had moved to Harlingen for repairs and returned to service by 19 March. She was soon renamed **Zwartewater** and, as such, had the distinction of being the last vessel in most alphabetical lists of coaster names. She was renamed **Oostzee** in 1995 and retained this name following sale to Latvian owners in October 2005.

(John Brownhill)

As the number of yards still building coastal vessels seems to become ever smaller, it can be a challenge to find a builder which is not mentioned elsewhere in the book. Although the Damen shipyard in Gorinchem is well-known, but not necessarily for building coasters, the builders of the hull of this ship are certainly not well-known. It was Liesbosch Staal B.V. in Nieuwegein that built the hull with completion taking place at Gorinchem. Nieuwegein is about five miles (eight kilometres) south of Utrecht and has been developed as a new town since 1971, catering for the growing population of Utrecht. The **Sea Hawk** (BRB, 1959gt/89) was launched as **Christian R** on 1 September 1989 but entered service as **Mindful**. She was sold and renamed **Christa K** in 1999 and became **Sea Hawk** following purchase by Northern Coasters Ltd and Kirkbylane Investments Ltd. Grimsby-based Torbulk Ltd are managers with Gillie & Blair looking after commercial management. We see her arriving at Princes Dock in Glasgow on 1 December with steel sections for a new footbridge to be built over the River Clyde. She was the second vessel to bring these sections from Invergordon and only the third commercial caller in Princes Dock during the current millennium.

(Barry Watson)

The **Cailin** (VCT, 2120gt/81) is one of three similar ships built at the Rauma-Repola shipyard in Uusikaupunki for the Russian government-owned merchant fleet. Originally named **Kapitan Voolens** and allocated to the Estonian Shipping Company, in 1992 she became **Kapten Voolens** when she was acquired by Estonian owners following the collapse of the Soviet Union in the previous year and subsequent dispersal of its merchant fleet. In 2003, she was sold to owners in a different Baltic state, namely Latvia, and was renamed **Cailin**. We see her at Montrose on 2 December.

(Barry Standerline)

Photography in Scotland can be challenging, with the sea lochs often seeming to have their individual weather systems. Holy Loch, which flows into the northern side of the Clyde near Dunoon, evidently had low cloud on 4 December as the **Alholmen** (FIN, 2580gt/84) arrived to load a part-cargo of round timber at Sandbank's marina pier. She later sailed to Kyle where she loaded the balance of her cargo for delivery to Rauma in Finland. A product of the Nieuwe Noord Nederlandse shipyard in Groningen, she was built to the maximum dimensions of the Trollhätte Canal in Sweden and was operated as **Mangen** by Ahlmark Lines, based in Karlstad on Lake Vänern, whose ships are frequent users of the Trollhätte Canal as they deliver cargoes of round timber and take away finished timber products. She was acquired by Finnish owners and renamed **Alholmen** in mid-April 2007.

(Charlie McCurdy)

The arrival of a Turkish ship in the River Trent would be noteworthy in itself; the arrival of this ship on 18 December was especially noteworthy because of the ship's history. Of 1557gt, she was launched at the Nordsøværftet shipyard in Ringkøbing as **Arktis Pearl** on 22 June 1984 and delivered on 29 August to Copenhagen-based Elite Shipping. In July 2001 she was sold to owners in Singapore and on 2 October was delivered to her new owners by whom she was renamed **Feng Shun Union** under the flag of St Vincent and the Grenadines. Her name was later written as **Fengshun Union**. In April 2004, she was bought by Chinese owners and renamed **Dong Yuan** under the Chinese flag. After trading in the Far East for two years, the next stage in her career saw her bought by Turkish owners in July 2006. Renamed **S. Hacibekiroglu** and transferred back to the St Vincent flag, she remained in the Far East for a further two months and did not arrive at Tuzla until 25 November 2006. Flying the flag of Panama since March 2008, she was photographed as she approached Flixborough wharf at the end of a voyage from Bilbao.

(Simon Smith)

Apart from fishing vessels and a motley collection of workboats, the *Amada* (PRK, 995gt/71) was the only vessel seen at the Greek port of Kalamata on 23 December. She had been abandoned and is believed to have been idle at the port for some time. She was built at the Kramer & Booy shipyard at Kootstertille where she was launched as *Hela* for a Bremen-based company on 27 March 1971. In 1972, she was renamed *Portainer* and reverted to her original name in 1980. Later changes of identity saw her become *Maria von Barssel* (1984), *Inge* (1988), *Heidi* (1989), *Karteria* (1997), *Ria* (1999) and *Amada* (2003).

(Nigel Jones)

The *Scot Pioneer* (2528gt/06) is yet another example of a modern Dutch coaster built at the prolific Peters shipyard in Kampen. Her hull was built at the Leda shipyard in Korcula, Croatia, and she was completed at Kampen. She is the third ship in the "Ice-Runner 3650" class and was built for Kustvaart Harlingen, a go-ahead company owned by four young Dutch captains. On 13 December 2006, she was named *Harns* by Sanne Boere, aged three, the daughter of Captain Arno Boere who is one of the partners in Kustvaart Harlingen. Indeed, he was in command for the ship's maiden voyage from Harlingen to Finland with a cargo of salt. Her name, incidentally, is the Frisian name of Harlingen. In early 2008 she was sold to Scotline and, renamed *Scot Pioneer*, was handed over in Harlingen on 9 March 2008. We see her arriving at Workington with a cargo of round timber on 27 December, having spent Christmas Day in Glasgow.

(Derek McAlone)

As the 2008 volume draws to a close we look at a final two coastal tankers, neither of which was constructed in Turkey. The *Navajo* (MLT, 2440gt/02) was built in South Korea at the Samho shipyard in Tong Young (sometimes rendered as Tongyong). This shipyard was established in 1994 and was then known as the Huedong shipyard. In 1996 it delivered its first 5000dwt chemical tanker to overseas buyers and became Samho shipyard in June 2001. It has concentrated on the construction of chemical and gas tankers and cement carriers. We see the *Navajo* in the Gilbrook Basin at Birkenhead on 27 December.

(Darren B Hillman)

As tanker operators combine to form ever-larger companies, the names of traditional owners tend to disappear. In 2005, the Clipper Group which had already taken over the UK's Crescent Tankships Ltd merged with Wonsild Tankers A/S to become Clipper Wonsild. It was not long before the familiar green hulls of Wonsild vessels started to be repainted into the dark blue of Clipper and the word Wonsild disappeared from ship names in favour of Clipper. Despite this, there are still some Wonsild names and colours to be seen. On 28 December, the *Frances Wonsild* (ITA, 2349gt/94) passes Calshot at the start of a voyage to Rotterdam from No. 7 Berth at the Fawley oil terminal. She was built at the Soc. Esercizio shipyard in Viareggio.

(Phil Kempsey)

Index of ship names

Name	Page	Name	Page	Name	Page
Alacrity	5	*Frelon*	36	*Potosi*	15
Alholmen	53	*Freyja*	20	*Princessa Arktiki*	31
Amada	54	*Fri Star*	34	*Priscilla*	48
Anina	50	*Gullfjord*	28	*Red Duchess*	51
Antares	8	*Hajo*	41	*Rig*	11
Arctic Princess	31	*Hanne Theresa*	4	*RMS Kiel*	6
Arklow Sky	2	*Harvest Caroline*	18	*RMS Snowlark*	20
Arngast	26	*Henny*	19	*RMS Vindava*	35
Ashley	46	*Hertfordshire*	10	*RMS Wedau*	43
Atlantis Alvarado	17	*Hydra*	4	*S. Hacibekiroglu*	53
Avant	12	*Imel Abdena*	29	*Saffier*	7
Baltic Breeze 1	34	*Ingunn*	24	*Samy*	31
Baltic Sky	38	*Irafoss*	13	*Scot Pioneer*	54
Barentszzee	35	*Jade*	48	*Sea Hawk*	52
Bawa I	38	*Jana*	23	*Sea Ruby*	36
Bellona	21	*Kaptain Salih*	22	*Seacement 1*	28
Bravery	39	*Karim*	39	*Selene Prahm*	7
Bremer Elena	41	*Korsika*	21	*Shetland Trader*	3
Cailin	52	*Kumkale*	19	*Sommen*	17
Carrier	37	*Lider Ceylan*	22	*Steenborg*	30
Celtic Endeavour	8	*Liva Greta*	11	*Swedica Hav*	3
Celtic Voyager	18	*Marte*	24	*Tege*	26
Cemsea	40	*Maya*	43	*Torpo*	50
Clipper Beaune	6	*Merel V*	32	*Trans Agila*	16
Coastal Deniz	15	*Merit*	45	*Tulos*	33
Coral Sea	47	*Michelle*	29	*Union Mercury*	14
Curlew	47	*Monika*	25	*Uno*	32
Diamant	10	*Navajo*	55	*Vadero Highlander*	44
Doris K	33	*Neptun*	9	*Vassilios XV*	44
Edro II	42	*Olga*	49	*Vedrey Hallarna*	5
Eider	12	*Oostzee*	51	*Vermland*	49
Elbetor	47	*Paganini*	37	*Vestland*	40
Elifnaz G	23	*Pardi*	45	*Vitali Kozhin*	25
Erlanda	27	*Patri*	16	*Whitspray*	9
Fjordtank	13	*Paula*	27	*Wotan*	42
Flinterbothnia	14	*Polla Rose*	46		
Frances Wonsild	55	*Pommern*	30		

Author's note

As far as possible, the outline history of each ship is given for the benefit of readers who may wish to research the ships featured in more detail and possibly to aid recognition of a ship perhaps seen under a previous name. In common with other shipping books, I have included details of the flag flown by the ship at the time of the photograph, along with gross tonnage figure and year of build. These statistics are the latest available at the time of writing. For various reasons, tonnage figures can vary according to the source used and because the ships themselves are subject to remeasurement. The figures given, therefore, should not be considered as definitive. Flag abbreviations are as below. The location of some of the ports and shipyards mentioned in the text may not be familiar to all readers. No attempt is made to further define these locations - extra research ought to be part of the enjoyment derived from this book!

Contributions in the form of prints, transparencies or digital images, are welcomed for further volumes in this series. Please ensure that your name is written on photographic material, along with outline details of the ship, location and date of the photograph. Any further information which could be used in a caption is welcome.

Flag abbreviations

ANT	Netherlands Antilles	GIB	Gibraltar	NOR	Norway
ATG	Antigua and Barbuda	GRC	Greece	PAN	Panama
BHS	Bahamas	IOM	Isle of Man	PRK	North Korea
BLZ	Belize	ITA	Italy	RUS	Russia
BRB	Barbados	JAM	Jamaica	SLE	Sierra Leone
CYM	Cayman Islands	KHM	Cambodia	SWE	Sweden
CYP	Cyprus	LTU	Lithuania	SVK	Slovakia
DEU	Germany	LVA	Latvia	TUR	Turkey
DIS	Danish International Register	MLT	Malta	VCT	St Vincent and the Grenadines
DMA	Dominica	NIS	Norwegian International Register		
DNK	Denmark				
FIN	Finland	NLD	Netherlands		

No separate identifying letters are given to British ships in this book.

Back cover top : The western side of the West Pier at Whitstable has become popular as a lay-by and repair berth. Noted there at the start of 2008 was the **Lark** (794gt/84), ex **Hoo Laurel**-06. Owned by Coastal Bulk Shipping Ltd, there will be more information about this fleet on page 47.

(Kevin Bassett)

Back cover bottom : Attempts by photographers in northern Europe to obtain a good photograph on New Year's Eve were thwarted by cloud cover almost everywhere. Thankfully one of our regular contributors was enjoying sunshine in Las Palmas and he noted the much-renamed **Kryst-I** (PAN, 2892gt/76) leaving port. Built by "Friesland" BV at Lemmer, she was launched on 30 June 1976 and delivered to her Dutch owners as **Annette** on 30 September. She was operated by the Holwerda group in her early years and was renamed **Samsun Dawn** in 1983 and **Frisian Dawn** in 1985. This sequence of quick name changes continued through the mid-1980s and saw her become **Lemsterland** in 1986 and **Evangelia II** in the following year after sale to Cypriot-flag operators. After moving to Mediterranean trade, she was renamed **Evan** in 1995, **Annette** in 2000 and **Kryst-I** in 2001. She now trades regularly between Spain, Morocco and the Canary Islands.

(Martin Penwright)